Pine Road Library
Lower Moreland Township
Huntington Valley, Pa.

WHAT MAKES A FISH?

THE ANIMAL KINGDOM

Lynn M. Stone

The Rourke Book Co., Inc.
Vero Beach, Florida 32964

© 1997 The Rourke Book Co., Inc.

All rights reserved. No part of this book may be reproduced or utilized in any form or by any means, electronic or mechanical including photocopying, recording or by any information storage and retrieval system without permission in writing from the publisher.

PHOTO CREDITS
Cover, pages 4, 7, 8, 13, 15, 17 © Marty Snyderman; pages 12, 21 © Breck P. Kent; title page, pages 10, 18, © Lynn M. Stone

EDITORIAL SERVICES:
Penworthy Learning Systems

Library of Congress Cataloging-in-Publication Data

Stone, Lynn M.
    What Makes a Fish? / by Lynn M. Stone.
      p. cm. — (The Animal Kingdom)
    Includes index
    Summary: Discusses the habits, bodies, and different kinds of fish and their relationships with people.
    ISBN 1-55916-193-0
    1. Fish—Juvenile literature. [1. Fish] I. Title II. Series: Stone, Lynn M. Animal Kingdom
QL617.2.S73 1997
597—dc21   96–52115
                                                                                                             CIP
                                                                                                             AC

Printed in the USA

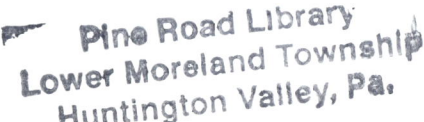

TABLE OF CONTENTS

Fish	5
Habits of Fish	6
Kinds of Fish	9
Where Fish Live	11
Bodies of Fish	14
Amazing Fish	16
Predator and Prey	19
Baby Fish	20
People and Fish	22
Glossary	23
Index	24

FISH

Several groups of animals—fish, amphibians, reptiles, birds, and mammals—have backbones.

Fish differ in one or more ways from each of the other groups. Fish have fins, live in water, and usually have scales. Almost all **species** (SPEE sheez), or kinds, of fish breathe through **gills** (GILZ) instead of lungs.

Like reptiles and amphibians, fish are **cold-blooded** (KOLD BLUD ed). Their body temperature is close to that of the water around them.

Whales live in the water, but they are mammals. They breathe air and they are warm-blooded.

Fins and scales help separate fish from other groups of animals with backbones.

HABITS OF FISH

Most fish are active swimmers. They travel to find food, a hiding place, or a place to lay eggs.

Many fish species live in large groups called **schools** (SKOOLZ). Others live by themselves.

Some fish make long journeys. Pacific salmon, for example, travel from far at sea to the freshwater rivers where they were born. There they lay their eggs and die.

A few kinds of fish never leave their little corner of the pond or ocean.

A large school of snappers glides through warm sea in search of food.

KINDS OF FISH

Scientists know of about 22,000 species of fish. Most of them have skeletons of bone.

Another major group has skeletons made mostly of **cartilage** (KAHR tl ij). The frame of your nose is made of cartilage. Cartilage is strong, but it bends and it is lighter than bone.

About 1,800 kinds of fish, including sharks and rays, belong to the cartilage family.

Bat ray and its cousins have skeletons made mostly of lightweight cartilage instead of bone.

WHERE FISH LIVE

Fish of one kind or another live almost anywhere there is water. Fish even live among the icebergs of the Arctic and Antarctic seas.

Most species live in the oceans. Still, more than 8,000 kinds of fish live in freshwater rivers, lakes, hot springs, and mud pools.

Some fish live in a mixture of fresh and salt water. Others travel back and forth, between fresh and salt water.

Pacific salmon are born in fresh water, but grow up at sea. Certain eels are born at sea, but grow up in rivers.

Red salmon from the sea return to a freshwater stream in British Columbia, Canada, to lay their eggs.

Pan-shaped flounder hides against rocky sea bottom.

Eels have unusual, snakelike shapes, but they're fish.

BODIES OF FISH

A fish's body is shaped to help it survive in its own way. Fast-swimming fish, like tunas, for example, have torpedo shapes. Fish that live and lie on the ocean bottom are often plate-shaped.

Most fish bodies are smooth, slimy, and streamlined. Their color matches their surroundings in the water. Some fish are as brightly colored as candy canes. Others look like seaweed.

Shark's torpedo shape helps it swim easily.

AMAZING FISH

Fish are amazing for many reasons. The whale shark, for example, is the world's largest fish. It grows more than 40 feet (12 meters) long. Yet it lives on tiny, floating plants and animals called **plankton** (PLANGK tun).

The walking catfish can move over land by using its fins like feet. Some fish make their own light deep in the ocean where sunlight can't reach.

A few fish can breathe air. A few other species can "fly" by skipping across the ocean surface.

Diver swims with a huge whale shark, the world's largest fish.

PREDATOR AND PREY

As adults, most fish are **predators** (PRED uh terz). They catch other animals, or **prey** (PRAY), for food. Certain sharks, bluefish, piranhas, and barracudas are among the predator fish.

Predator fish usually eat other fish. Great white sharks, however, kill seals. A few fish eat clams and other hard-shelled creatures.

Few fish live only on a diet of plants. Many fish eat plankton, the mix of tiny plants and animals.

Fish are prey for snakes, pelicans, eagles, herons, otters, seals, and many other animals.

Fish are prey for many animals. This brown bear has caught a salmon in Alaska.

BABY FISH

Fish hatch from eggs. The female fish lays her eggs in water. Eggs may drift, or the female may lay them in a "nest."

Salmon make saucer-like scrapes in stream bottoms as nests for their eggs.

Some fish species have eggs that hatch inside the mothers. These fish, including the great white shark, bear their young alive.

Baby fish, or **fry** (FRY), may look much like their parents—or they may look almost nothing like adult fish.

Newly hatched rainbow trout will live on its egg yolk for a short time.

PEOPLE AND FISH

Fish are important both as predators and prey. They help preserve the balance of nature. Healthy lakes, rivers, and oceans are important for people as well as animals.

Fish are important to people for food and sport, too. Fishing boats catch thousands of pounds of fish. Fish farms raise salmon, trout, catfish, and carp.

Many kinds of wild fish have become scarce because of pollution and too much fishing.

Glossary

cartilage (KAHR tl ij) — the strong, flexible body tissue that makes up most of a shark's or ray's skeleton

cold-blooded (KOLD BLUD ed) — refers to animals whose body temperature stays about the same as that of their surroundings fish, amphibians, and reptiles

fry (FRY) — small, young fish

gills (GILZ) — organs that help fish and certain other animals breathe by taking oxygen from water

plankton (PLANGK tun) — tiny, floating plants and animals of the sea and other bodies of water

predator (PRED uh ter) — an animal that hunts other animals for food

prey (PRAY) — an animal that is hunted by another animal for food

school (SKOOL) — a group of fish swimming together

species (SPEE sheez) — within a group of closely related animals, one certain kind, such as a *rainbow* trout

INDEX

cartilage   9
catfish, walking   16
eels   11
eggs   6, 20
fins   5
fish   5, 6, 9, 11, 14, 16, 19, 20, 22
   bodies of   14
   species of   5, 9
fry   20
gills   5
nests   20
oceans   6, 11, 22
people   22
plankton   16, 19
predator   19, 22

prey   19, 22
rays   9
rivers   6, 11, 22
salmon   6, 11, 20, 22
scales   5
schools   6
skeletons   9
sharks   9, 19
   great white   19, 20
   whale   16
tuna   14
whales   5